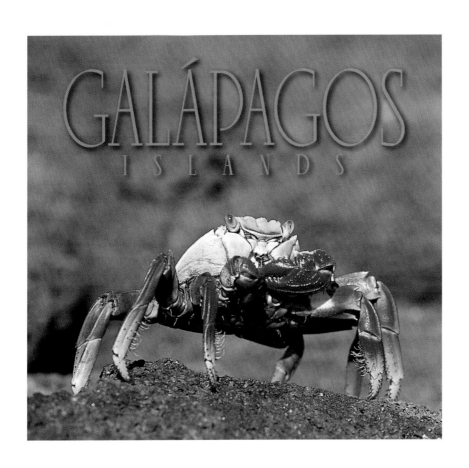

GALÁPAGOS
ISLANDS

NATURE'S DELICATE
BALANCE AT RISK

LINDA TAGLIAFERRO

LERNER PUBLICATIONS COMPANY
MINNEAPOLIS

To my husband, Fred Thorner, for listening to all my stories about marine iguanas and Lonesome George.

Acknowledgments
I would like to thank all the people who helped me with information for this book, especially Mary Winget, my patient editor; Johannah Barry, executive director of the Charles Darwin Foundation in Falls Church, Virginia; Dr. Linda Cayot, former coordinator of the Isabela Project at the Charles Darwin Research Station, Santa Cruz, Galápagos Islands; Dr. Carlos Valle, Professor of Ecology and Conservation Biology at the University of San Francisco de Quito, Ecuador; Dr. Edward Louis, geneticist at the Henry Doorly Zoo in Omaha, Nebraska; the Public Relations Department at the San Diego Zoo; Dr. Matthew James of the Galápagos Coalition; Dr. Tom Fritts, research biologist; John Woram, Galápagos Islands fan extraordinaire; Dr. Martin Wikelski; and everyone else who made this book possible.

Lerner Publications Company
A division of Lerner Publishing Group
241 First Avenue North
Minneapolis, MN 55401 U.S.A.

Website address: www.lernerbooks.com

LIBRARY OF CONGRESS CATALOGING-IN-PUBLICATION DATA

Tagliaferro, Linda.
    Galápagos Islands : nature's delicate balance at risk / Linda Tagliaferro.
       p.   cm.
    Includes bibliographical references and index.
    ISBN 0-8225-0648-3 (lib. bdg. : alk. paper)
    1. Zoology—Galápagos Islands—Juvenile literature. 2. Animal ecology—Galápagos Islands—Juvenile literature. 3. Galápagos Islands—Juvenile literature. [1. Galápagos Islands. 2. Zoology—Galápagos Islands. 3. Animal ecology. 4. Ecology.] I. Title.
    QL345.G2 T34 2001
    591.9866'5—dc21   00-009781

Manufactured in the United States of America
1 2 3 4 5 6 – JR – 06 05 04 03 02 01

Contents

INTRODUCTION: Islands of Wonder

Imagine that you are having a dream about some far-off islands where everything seems magical. Strange, wonderful animals and plants surround you. Volcanoes loom in the distance. Cactus plants grow as tall as trees, and much of the ground is twisted and folded from dried lava.

You take a few halting steps in this dreamlike landscape, and you see a huge tortoise—almost 5 feet long, weighing more than 600 pounds. You turn around, and a bird the size of a sparrow boldly flies straight toward you and begins to pull on your shoelaces with its delicate bill. You walk to the water's edge and watch white birds with big blue webbed feet waddle past you and then dive into the ocean in search of a quick meal. You dive into the water after the bird, and you're suddenly surrounded by friendly sea lions that jump and frolic as they swim in circles around you.

If you think such things couldn't possibly happen in real life, you're wrong. All these amazing events take place on the Galápagos Islands in the Pacific Ocean.

The islands are home to an amazing variety of different species, or kinds, of plants and animals. From the smallest birds to the largest sea lions, none of the animals in this island group fears humans. This treasure trove of biodiversity—or wide variety of life-forms—has fascinated both scientists and tourists for centuries. Scientists are still discovering new creatures on these islands and in the surrounding waters.

Dried lava formed the Galápagos Islands, including the island of Bartolomé (left). A waning sunset falls behind the island's black hills.

Charles Darwin was a naturalist and a leader in the field of biological science. While visiting the Galápagos Islands, he conducted studies on the islands' wildlife. He published his conclusions in a book of essays titled On the Origin of Species *in 1859.*

The Galápagos inspired one nineteenth-century scientist, Charles Darwin, to come up with a theory that revolutionized the way we think plant and animal species develop. The islands are among the last places on earth that contain so many uncommon organisms in such a small area.

To learn more about the Galápagos Islands is to learn how life functions on our planet. To appreciate the natural wonders on these incredible islands is to understand why we must conserve the many amazing and exotic life-forms that thrive in the Galápagos.

On Santa Fé Island, opuntia cactuses grow as tall as trees. The Galápagos are filled with forms of vegetation found nowhere else in the world.

Chapter 1

Swept Away to the Magical Islands

In 1535 Fray Tomás de Berlanga, the bishop of Panama, set sail across the Pacific Ocean for Peru, South America, but landed instead in a strange and unexpected destination. Ocean currents had carried his ship far off course to a group of mysterious islands in the Pacific Ocean.

Spanish sailors originally called the islands where the bishop and his crew anchored "Las Islas Encantadas," which is Spanish for "the Enchanted Isles." The sailors thought the islands were bewitched because navigation around this area was difficult and frequently dangerous. The strong and changeable currents that surround the islands made sailing in the archipelago—or chain of islands—a great risk. The islands often seemed to disappear into the fog, so early navigators falsely concluded that the islands themselves were moving and could float freely around the Pacific. The Galápagos Islands are still considered strange and unusual by some, but conservationists and others who value nature view them as an enormous treasure in a world faced with mass extinction of unique plants and animals.

Since the bishop was swept away to his unexpected discovery, many visitors have come to the magical archipelago. Pirates, whalers, and scientists have sailed to this destination, either to steal or to study the natural wealth that abounds there.

The Galápagos Islands were first discovered by humans in the 1500s, when explorers and pirates sailed around the world in ships like this Spanish galleon.

Gone Forever

When a plant or animal species becomes extinct, all of its kind has died out. The species will never live again. Some extinct animals died out gradually because of changes in their environment, such as a rise or fall in temperatures. Other species were lost because of pollution or because their habitat was destroyed. Some were even hunted to extinction.

No one knows for sure why the dinosaurs died out, but many scientists think that environmental changes caused these animals to disappear from the earth. All that is left are skeletons.

As late as the nineteenth century, millions of birds called passenger pigeons *(below left)* lived in the midwestern United States. Some people liked the taste of these birds, however, and hunters killed so many that by 1914 the last passenger pigeon had died.

Probably the most famous extinct animal is the dodo *(above right)*, a species of bird that once lived on Mauritius, an island in the Indian Ocean. These large birds weighed about 50 pounds and had blue-gray feathers, large bills, and small, weak wings. Unable to fly and unafraid of humans, these birds were easy prey for the Portuguese sailors who landed on the island in the 1500s. The sailors killed and ate many of them. Others became extinct because the Portuguese sailors introduced rats and pigs that destroyed the nests and eggs of these birds. By 1681 the last of the dodos had died.

We must learn from these sad examples. Everyone should be concerned about preserving the great natural treasures that remain on this earth and make sure that they do not die out because of humankind's actions.

The challenge that modern conservationists face is how to preserve the islands so nature can continue to work its magic throughout the archipelago. They must find ways to prevent the archipelago from being ruined by too many tourists and others who could change the original, unspoiled beauty and biodiversity of the area.

Magical Islands in the Sun

The Galápagos Islands lie on the equator, about 600 miles west of Ecuador, the South American country that has owned them since 1832. Thirteen major islands and many smaller ones lie in a 200-square-mile area in the Pacific Ocean. The largest island, Isabela, measures 75 miles at its longest point. Other major islands include Fernandina, San Cristóbal, San Salvador, and Santa Cruz.

Despite the archipelago's location on the equator, the waters surrounding the Galápagos are relatively cool, averaging 72 degrees Fahrenheit. This unusually low temperature results from the Humboldt Current, the strong flow of ocean waters that starts in Antarctica and continues north along the Pacific coast of South America. Just below the equator, the current changes course to the west, bringing cool waters to the Galápagos.

This cooler water brings many blessings with it. There is an abundance of marine life-forms, including countless varieties of fish and sea vegetation that can survive only in lower temperatures. As a result, the waters surrounding the islands are a paradise for birds such as boobies, petrels, and tropic birds, which are all seafood eaters. Without this steady supply of ocean food, the birds could not survive.

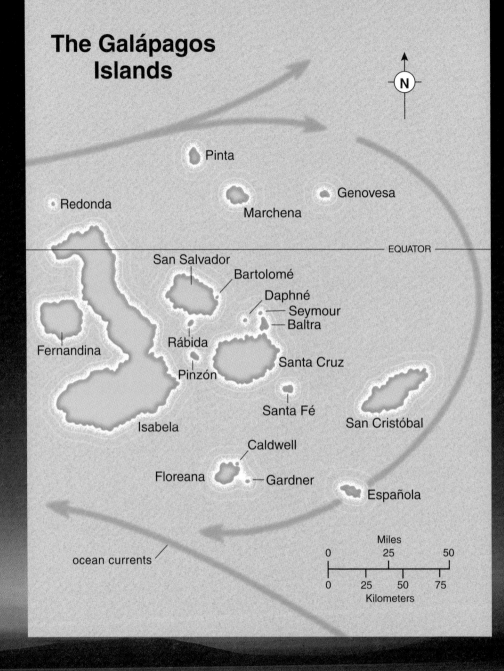

The Galápagos Islands

Pinta

Redonda

Marchena

Genovesa

EQUATOR

San Salvador

Bartolomé

Daphné

Seymour

Baltra

Fernandina

Rábida

Pinzón

Santa Cruz

Santa Fé

San Cristóbal

Isabela

Caldwell

Floreana

Gardner

Española

ocean currents

N

Miles

0   25   50

0   25   50   75

Kilometers

Fire in the Ocean

Born out of massive undersea volcanic activity that occurred millions of years ago, the Galápagos are geologically similar to Hawaii. Lava slowly and steadily built up underwater until it formed undersea mountains. As lava continued to build up, the tops of these formations jutted above the water as islands.

One theory about the geological origin of these islands sug gests that they formed above what is called a hot spot—an area in the mantle of the earth that contains more heat than others. The mantle is the layer of the earth above the core of our planet. Above the mantle is the crust, the outer rocky layer of the earth. The crust is divided into a number of sections called tectonic plates. These plates float on top of the mantle and can move up to an inch or more every year. Some of the plates are so large that they can encompass an entire continent.

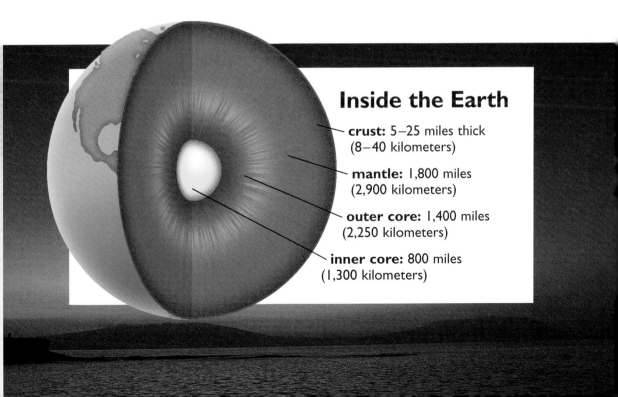

Inside the Earth

crust: 5–25 miles thick (8–40 kilometers)

mantle: 1,800 miles (2,900 kilometers)

outer core: 1,400 miles (2,250 kilometers)

inner core: 800 miles (1,300 kilometers)

The Galápagos Islands lie over a spot where three tectonic plates—the Cocos, the Pacific, and the Nazca Plates—come together. As this area came in contact with a hot spot far below the Pacific Ocean, the mantle and crust in that area heated up so intensely that the crust finally melted. Molten lava escaped from the earth's core and traveled to the surface.

Eventually, an island formed and extended above the water. As the tectonic plates moved, this island was slowly pushed eastward. Then a new area of the earth's crust came in contact with the hot spot, and this in turn formed another island. This process repeated itself over millions of years until all the islands in the archipelago were formed.

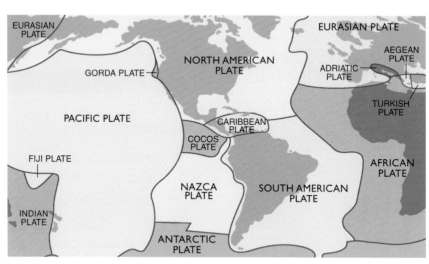

The earth's crust is made up of tectonic plates consisting of crust and part of the mantle. The plates move slowly on a layer of hot rock in the mantle, carrying the continents and the ocean floor with them.

The oldest islands are estimated to be from three to four-and-a-half million years old. The youngest island, Fernandina, which lies in the western end of the archipelago, may have formed about seven hundred thousand years ago. Although they were created long ago, the Galápagos Islands are considered relatively young by geologists' standards, and the archipelago is still in a slow, persistent state of change.

Nature's Treasures

Despite their similarity to places like Hawaii, the archipelago is not just another group of islands in paradise. The Galápagos Islands are important to us because they are among the few places left where nature has been allowed to run its unspoiled course. They are home to many species of flora and fauna, or plants and animals, that are endemic, or found nowhere else on earth. Almost all of the land reptiles are endemic, and 75 percent of the land birds in the Galápagos are also unique to the islands.

This biodiversity is a natural treasure that must be preserved. The islands are home to the only penguins found outside of frigid waters, giant tortoises that can weigh hundreds of pounds, and opuntia cactuses—which grow to the height of immense trees and provide food, water, and sometimes even shelter for some exotic animals that live in this archipelago. Swallow-tailed gulls (the only nocturnal seagulls in the world) and flightless cormorants (small-winged, earthbound versions of a species that usually take to the sky) inhabit the Galápagos. Scalesia trees, distant relatives of sunflowers, grow to heights of 60 feet in these islands.

In 1996 an expedition sponsored by the Discovery Channel,

The Galápagos penguin is one species of the rare birds that live on the islands. These penguins look out to sea while Sally Lightfoot crabs crawl around lava rocks.

one of the largest cable networks in the United States, resulted in a television program called "Galápagos: Beyond Darwin." A team of researchers went as deep as 3,000 feet underwater in a submersible vehicle called the Johnson Sea Link to study previously unexplored ocean depths surrounding the islands.

Researchers discovered several dozen new species of deep-sea creatures, including two types of jellyfish and deep-sea moray eels. They also discovered a deepwater red octopus that lives 1,500 feet below the ocean's surface.

Among the extremely rare species discovered on this expedition were the viperfish, which has razor-sharp fangs to catch its prey, and the Galápagos four-eyed blenny. This endemic fish can see and even breathe outside of water. It can wiggle over 100 feet onto land in search of an insect meal.

The Voyage of the *Beagle*

These islands are also unique due to their lack of people. The small human population on the Galápagos only inhabits some of the main islands: Santa Cruz, San Cristóbal, Floreana (also known as Santa Maria), Isabela, and Baltra. Elsewhere, animals live and roam freely. Visitors to the islands are struck by the tameness of the animals. Sea lions swim out as the "welcoming committee" when tourists come ashore from their cruise ships. Birds fearlessly fly down to humans many times their size, and land iguanas casually amble past groups of tourists.

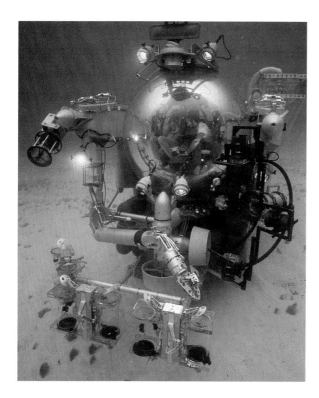

The Johnson Sea Link allows scientists to explore underwater near the Galápagos Islands.

Some famous visitors experienced the wonder of these islands. One was Herman Melville (1819–1891), the author of *Moby Dick* and other well-known stories. He once worked aboard a whaling ship that anchored in the Galápagos. His short story "Las Encantadas" paints a dismal portrait of the islands as barren and inhospitable.

Perhaps the most famous visitor to the archipelago was Charles Darwin (1809–1882). The British scientist's five-year voyage as resident naturalist on a ship called the HMS *Beagle* eventually changed the course of his life and led to an astounding theory that rocked the scientific community of his time. In 1835 the *Beagle* stopped in the Galápagos. Darwin noticed that each island had plants and animals that were different from those on the other islands in the archipelago. He also noted

Charles Darwin sailed to the Galápagos Islands on the HMS Beagle, *shown in the drawing above.*

that many of the Galápagos varieties had close relatives living on the mainland of South America. But how could they have traveled hundreds of miles to the islands?

He observed different types of Galápagos finches, which are known in modern times as Darwin's finches. He noticed that finches on different islands had different types of bills. For instance, the medium ground finch has a strong bill that can easily crack open seeds, whereas the small tree finch has one that is less powerful and more suited to eating insects. It seemed to Darwin that each finch's bill was well suited to the food that could be found on the island where the finch lived.

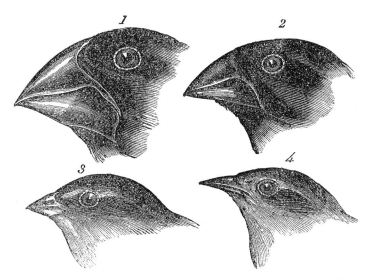

Charles Darwin's drawings of four finches (1. large ground finch, 2. medium ground finch, 3. small tree finch, and 4. warbler finch) appeared in his book A Naturalist's Voyage: Journal of Researches into the Natural History and Geology of the Countries Visited during the Voyage of HMS Beagle *around the World. Darwin's observations of the different bills and eating habits of finches around the Galápagos Islands contributed to his theory of natural selection.*

In 1859, more than twenty years after the *Beagle*'s voyage, Charles Darwin published his book *On the Origin of Species,* which explained his theory of natural selection, or the survival of the fittest. This theory contradicted the theory of creationism, which holds that God's creatures have all remained as they were originally made on the day of creation. The theory of natural selection, on the other hand, states that all species of plants and animals are in a state of slow change because they are adapting to their physical surroundings.

Darwin said that if an individual animal or plant was well suited to a particular environment, then it would tend to thrive in this area and live long enough to reproduce. Its relatives that did not fit in well would tend to die out. Over time, the species would gradually change to fit its environment.

Trouble in Paradise

Almost all the other major archipelagos in the world have lost many of their natural wonders. Islands in the Caribbean, the Hawaiian Islands, Guam, and New Zealand and its neighboring islands have all suffered the extinction of 75 percent of their plants and animals. The Galápagos Islands have lost relatively few of their unique populations.

All is not well in the archipelago, however. Although the animals in this ocean paradise have no predators to fear, one species—humans—does threaten some of these unique inhabitants. People have introduced animals, such as dogs, cats, pigs, goats, and rats, that have developed into feral—or wild—populations on many of the islands. These new animals pose a serious threat to iguanas, tortoises, native birds, and other species.

Humans have introduced goats (such as these on Isabela Island) and other nonnative animals to the Galápagos. These animals endanger tortoises, birds, and other creatures.

In 1940 only six hundred people were living in the archipelago. Then in 1949, a major earthquake occurred in continental Ecuador. This prompted some Ecuadoreans whose homes had been destroyed to move to the Galápagos. This population expansion continued until the early 1970s and happened whenever droughts, more earthquakes, or other natural disasters occurred in Ecuador. The 1980s, however, marked a time when the human population on the islands skyrocketed. Much of this expansion was a result of the tourism industry, which led to

As this fishing boat brings fish to the water's surface, brown pelicans and frigate birds scavenge for food. The fishing industry attracts people from mainland Ecuador to the islands.

jobs on the islands. In 1997 approximately fifteen thousand people were living in the archipelago.

Troubled Waters

Some people have moved to the islands because of the fishing industry in the area. In 1988 a new fishery opened for sea cucumbers, large worm-shaped ocean creatures. Marine biologist David Pawson calls them "the earthworms of the sea." They are considered a delicacy in some Asian countries. The high prices paid by Asian buyers were an incentive for some poor Ecuadoreans to overfish this ecologically important species.

By 1992 the sea cucumber population was almost depleted. The government made it illegal to fish for this species in 1995. The *pepineros*—sea cucumber fishers—protested. They seized the offices of the Galápagos National Park and the Charles Darwin Research Station (CDRS) in Puerto Ayora on the island of Santa Cruz. Fifty angry pepineros took over the national park's office on Isabela Island. The conflicts continued, and in March 1997, a park warden from the Galápagos National Park Service (GNPS) was shot and seriously wounded during an investigation of an illegal pepinero camp on Isabela.

Saving the Ecosystem

Will tourism save the Galápagos by providing the money and awareness needed to support conservation efforts? Or will visitors and new residents to these islands contribute to the extinction of one-of-a-kind species of animals and plants? Research has shown that some species have already become extinct on this ecologically vulnerable archipelago.

The Galápagos is the only archipelago in the world that still has the majority of its plants and animals intact. It must be preserved so the islands can remain the "living laboratory of evolution," as some scientists have called them.

Chapter 2

Giants of the Land

The Galápagos Islands were named for some of their most famous inhabitants. In the early days of exploration, Spanish sailors were amazed at the size and tameness of the giant tortoises that roamed the area, so they called the site Las Islas Galápagos, or the "Tortoise Islands."

The government of Ecuador officially changed the name to Archipiélago de Colón, or Archipelago of Columbus, in 1892 to commemorate the four-hundredth anniversary of Columbus's voyage. (Christopher Columbus is called Cristóbal Colón in Spanish.) However, the name *Galápagos,* or Tortoise, became so popular that it continues to be used most often.

A tortoise is a reptile—a cold-blooded, egg-laying animal. It is a type of turtle that lives on land. A tortoise has stumpy legs that enable it to move around on solid ground with ease, as opposed to the webbed feet or flippers that are characteristic of water-based species such as sea turtles. The only places in the world where giant tortoises are found are the Galápagos Islands and Aldabra Island in the Indian Ocean, near Madagascar.

Male Galápagos tortoises, which are bigger than the females, can grow up to 6 feet in length and can weigh as much as 600 pounds. These tortoises reach their adult size in about twenty

Galápagos giant tortoises are extremely rare. They are descendants of reptiles that lived on the islands thousands of years ago.

years. After that point, they may continue to grow but do so more slowly. Newborn tortoises, which are called hatchlings, usually weigh less than ¼ pound.

In addition to their impressive size, the Galápagos tortoises are also amazing animals because they can live for such a long time. One giant tortoise was recorded to have lived for 152 years. Some scientists estimate that they can live even longer.

Scientists think that in the past, fourteen different tortoise subspecies—or smaller divisions of species—existed in the Galápagos, but only ten of these still exist. These different subspecies may have derived from a common ancestor and evolved separately on different islands as a result of factors such as the climate and plant life on the individual islands.

One theory states that smaller tortoises from South America could have drifted to the Galápagos on natural "rafts"—pieces of land that broke off from the continent during floods caused by heavy rainfall. The strong ocean currents could have carried the rafts to the islands. Scientists even think that it is possible for tortoises to float in the ocean without rafts and survive long voyages, because they can go without food or water for months at a time.

Domes and Saddles

All of the subspecies of giant tortoises in the Galápagos Islands fall into two general categories. The major difference between the two categories is the shape of the animals' carapace, or shell. One group of tortoises has a rounded, dome-shaped shell and a short neck. These tortoises are usually found on islands that have higher elevations where the giant creatures can eat grass and several types of abundant low-growing vegetation.

Galápagos giant tortoises
(above) *have a high, round
shell. Galápagos saddleback
tortoises* (right) *have a flatter
shell and longer legs and
neck. Both species of tortoises
are rare.*

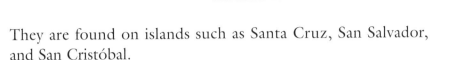

They are found on islands such as Santa Cruz, San Salvador, and San Cristóbal.

The other group of tortoises has a saddle-shaped carapace. These tortoises have long legs and a long neck, which are well suited for reaching up to feed on branches, grasses, or the fruits of the giant prickly pear cactus. Saddle-shaped tortoises are

Since the giant tortoises of the Galápagos Islands are not afraid of humans, photographers can walk right up to them.

found on Pinta and Española, islands that contain expanses of dry areas where vegetation is sparse.

Unnatural Predators

These gentle giants had no natural predators until the arrival of humans into their home. As a result, they show no fear of other animals or people. Tourists can walk up close to these slow-moving creatures without frightening them.

In the 1600s, pirates took advantage of the tortoises' lack of fear and removed huge numbers of them from the islands. These placid creatures were easy to catch because they are so slow-moving and passive. Because giant tortoises can survive without food or water for many months, they provided fresh meat for the seafaring adventurers. The pirates stacked the tortoises on top of one another in the ships' holds. Whenever meat was needed during the course of their long ocean journeys, the cooks would take some of the live animals and prepare them as hearty soups or stews for the hungry crew.

In the 1800s, thousands more of these shelled creatures were taken by whalers, who frequented the waters surrounding the islands. In 1831 sailors took thirteen thousand giant tortoises on board sixty-eight ships to provide fresh food. Giant tortoises were hunted to extinction on Floreana and Santa Fé. Fernandina had only one tortoise left in the early twentieth century, and it was unfortunately killed and collected by the 1905–1906 expedition of the California Academy of Sciences, the oldest scientific institution in the western United States.

Lonesome George

Of the eleven existing subspecies of tortoise, five are found on Isabela Island's volcanoes. Other subspecies exist on Santa Cruz, Española, Pinzón, San Cristóbal, and James. In 1971 one sole survivor of his subspecies was found on Pinta, and he was aptly named Lonesome George. This solitary male was brought to the CDRS on Santa Cruz in 1972 in the hope that he would one day mate with a surviving female of his own species.

Years later, researchers brought in two females from Volcan

Wolf—a major volcano on Isabela—to live with George in his enclosure. These tortoises are from a subspecies that seems the most physically similar to George's. However, since the tortoise has not attempted to mate with either of the females, and since it is highly unlikely that a female of his own subspecies exists on Pinta Island, some people fear that George's death will mark the end of his subspecies.

Searching DNA for George's Mate

Some scientists think that there is still hope for George's subspecies, however. Dr. Edward Louis, a geneticist at the Henry Doorly Zoo in Omaha, Nebraska, embarked on an ambitious project to reveal the mysteries of Lonesome George's background. In 1991 he began a project supervised by professors Jeremy Taylor and Scott Davis at Texas A&M University. The project proved so successful that it is ongoing.

Using new technologies that can analyze the DNA (deoxyribonucleic acid) of an organism, scientists can tell which species are closely related and which are not, even if they physically resemble each other. DNA is the molecule in all living things that carries the genetic code that gives organisms their special characteristics. DNA helps organisms produce exact copies of themselves. It has instructions for building many different kinds of cells.

Dr. Louis and his team went to the Galápagos and collected blood samples from all the wild populations of tortoises on San Cristóbal and Isabela. After the researchers collected blood samples and tested the DNA, they transferred the samples to a DNA bank in the United States. Studying the tortoises' DNA helped to clear up some misconceptions. In the past, some tortoises had been taken from the Galápagos and brought to zoos

Lonesome George is the last survivor of his subspecies of Galápagos giant tortoise. Modern science may help to make sure that his subspecies doesn't become extinct.

around the world. When these animals were returned to the Galápagos, no one knew which islands they had originally come from. As a result of the DNA testing, Dr. Louis and his team could pinpoint exactly where these tortoises had been born.

Dr. Louis explained that one major goal of his team's project was to find a mate for Lonesome George since no females could be found on Pinta, where George was born. So far, they have had no luck, but he added, "I think there's hope. There are still a lot of animals that we haven't looked at. We've sampled most of the wild-caught Galápagos tortoises [those that were caught on the islands] that are now in the United States, but internationally, there are a lot of other tortoises, and I'm sure we're going to get a lot more requests [to do DNA testing on them]."

In addition to Dr. Louis's work, another group of scientists helped to find out more about Lonesome George. In 1999 researchers at Yale University, the State University of New York in Syracuse, and the University of Rome in Italy conducted a study that led them to a surprising discovery. By studying the DNA of more than one hundred tortoises in the Galápagos, the researchers concluded that George's closest relations actually came from the islands of San Cristóbal and Española—far away from his native island of Pinta.

Darwin's Tortoise?

Among the wild-caught tortoises that live in zoos is a female tortoise captured on Santa Cruz. Her name is Harriet, and there is a theory that she might have been collected by Charles Darwin himself! Harriet lives in an Australian zoo, and positive documentation proves that she has been there since at least 1877. Dr. Louis has suggested that more research be done by checking newspapers from the 1800s to see if there is any mention of the date that Harriet was collected from the islands.

What would happen if Lonesome George mated with another species of tortoise? Dr. Louis said, "Even if he does breed with the closest population that he's related to, half that animal's genome [the total of all of its genes] is going to be George's. Natural selection is a very powerful force in the Galápagos, so if we could put George back on the island of Pinta and let natural selection do its thing, you might have little tortoises looking like Lonesome George one day."

Even if a suitable mate is found, however, it is still not certain whether George is capable of fathering a new family. Some scientists wonder if he is too old or too unhealthy to mate.

Trouble on Isabela

In the 1990s, researchers discovered that settlers who introduced domestic animals on Isabela created a problem affecting the giant tortoise population. Isabela, the largest island in the archipelago, is bigger than all the other Galápagos Islands combined. The lower section of the island has a town inhabited by people, and some farms are located there. When settlers arrived in the Galápagos in the 1800s, some of them imported goats as farm animals. Unfortunately, some of these goats escaped and quickly established themselves as a feral population.

Many introduced farm animals, such as horses, cattle, goats, dogs, and cats, have escaped and formed wild populations in the lower section of the island. What prevented them from going farther into the highlands was a stretch of volcanic rock that led to the higher pastures on Volcan Alcedo, the volcano that supports the largest populations of tortoises in the islands.

In 1979, however, some CDRS personnel discovered goats on the southern flanks of Alcedo. By 1990 there were more and more reports of goats arriving at the visitor site near Alcedo. A student working for the research station estimated that one or two thousand goats lived on Alcedo in the early 1990s, but by 1996 that estimate skyrocketed to between eighty thousand and one hundred thousand.

The highlands have what is known as *garua*, a thick fog that

In the Santa Cruz highlands, Galápagos giant tortoises and cattle walk quietly around each other. Domestic animals have greatly affected the lives of native animals.

comes in during the dry season, which usually runs from July to December. Garua often covers the southern rim of the volcano during those months. The trees in these areas are full of mosses, ferns, and other plants that collect water from the fog. The water drips down and creates pools, providing fresh water for the tortoises that congregate there.

It is estimated that in the dry season up to two thousand tortoises collect on the southern rim of Alcedo. Much to their dismay, researchers at the CDRS recently discovered that the goats have destroyed the vegetation that grew there. The once lush area is now open pasture with few trees. Only the scorching sun remains. The tortoises can no longer quench their thirst or find relief from the heat.

Born into Danger

Another problem for the giant tortoises is the many introduced species that threaten the hatchlings as soon as they emerge from their eggs. The mating season for the Galápagos tortoises usually begins in February and extends throughout March and

Giant tortoises are bred at the CDRS. This tortoise is hatching from its egg.

April. After a male and female have mated, the female makes the long, slow journey to a nesting site, which is usually far from the feeding grounds. She digs a nest with her hind legs and feet. Then she lays from 2 to 22 eggs that are about the size of tennis balls. Afterward, she puts a layer of mud mixed with her urine on top of the eggs to protect them.

These baby Galápagos tortoises are emerging from their nest.

About three months later, the baby tortoises emerge by breaking the eggshells with their movements. The babies use their claws and a special structure called an egg tooth—located on the top of their snout—to break through the shell.

These tiny hatchlings are inviting meals to a number of animals that people have introduced to the islands. Goats and wild pigs uproot the tortoise nests and eat the eggs and hatchlings. Rats, which were probably introduced by pirates centuries ago, also consume the eggs and young tortoises. Cattle and wild donkeys can destroy tortoise eggs by walking over the fragile nests.

Will feral animals eventually lead all the tortoises in the Galápagos to the same sad fate as Lonesome George's subspecies? The CDRS and the GNPS have instituted programs to reverse the destructive habits of feral animals so the islands can continue to be home to these wonderful slow-moving giants.

Chapter 3

Island Birds

Among the most fascinating inhabitants of the Galápagos skies are the frigate birds. Two species, the great frigate bird and the magnificent frigate bird, are present in the archipelago. Frigate birds measure up to 41 inches from head to tail, and they have pointed wings that give them the power to fly gracefully through the air.

The magnificent frigate bird, the larger of the two species, can have a wingspan as wide as 7 feet. Both types have a tail with a characteristic forked shape that can open and close like scissors. The tail helps the birds navigate the skies with ease and speed.

One theory holds that powerful seabirds, such as the frigate birds, came to the islands by flying from the mainland of South America. Along the way, they might have made stops on smaller islands or large rock formations that jut out of the Pacific Ocean. This theory makes sense in view of the fact that strong winds blow from the mainland to the Galápagos area. Even without these winds, however, frigate birds can fly long distances with their large, powerful wings.

The adult male great frigate birds have black plumage with a greenish sheen to it, while the adult male magnificent frigate birds have a purplish sheen to their feathers. Females of the two species are easier to identify. The great frigate females are black with white feathers from their chests to their chins. The

Frigate birds have forklike tails that can open and close.

The larger the great frigate bird's red throat sac, the more attractive he is to females of the species.

female magnificent frigate birds, in contrast, have white feathers that extend only to their throat.

The great frigate bird usually feeds in the Pacific Ocean surrounding the Galápagos Islands, often flying long distances from the shore. The magnificent frigate bird, however, is often found along the coasts and in the ocean between the islands. A frigate bird can hover over the water and swoop down swiftly to catch fish. It seems as if only its bill touches the water because it is so skillful at flying. There is a practical reason for the birds to avoid becoming wet. The birds' feathers are not completely waterproof, like those of ducks and other waterbirds. If frigate birds become totally immersed in water, they could drown.

Although frigate birds are found in other places in the world—such as Cocos Island (between Costa Rica and the Galápagos), tropical parts of the Atlantic, Pacific, and Indian Oceans, and the Caribbean Sea—the Galápagos is the only place in the world where both the great frigate bird and the magnificent frigate bird inhabit the same islands.

Stolen Suppers

Another unique aspect of the island's avian, or bird, population is that the magnificent frigate birds are known as "man-o'-war" birds. These pirates of the sky sometimes steal food from other birds in flight. They are especially skilled at stealing meals from boobies, seabirds that are common in the Galápagos. Noticing birds with a mouthful of freshly caught fish or other tempting meals, a magnificent frigate bird might pull at a booby's tail or peck at its wings until it drops its prey. Then the skillful magnificent frigate bird swoops down and steals the abandoned food. In the Galápagos, both kinds of male frigate birds mostly steal food in the air, but in the skies above the Caribbean Sea, the female frigate birds usually perform this type of theft.

Frigate birds also steal meals in an unappetizing way. This author saw a pelican regurgitate its food, only to have a frigate bird descend and eat the other bird's thrown-up meal.

Looking for Love in the Skies

Visitors to the great frigate bird colony on Genovesa Island in the Galápagos can never forget the sights and sounds of hundreds of male birds spread out over the landscape. These birds are not shy about wanting to be noticed. During the mating season, which is generally during the first half of the year, the gular sac, or throat sac, of these male birds gradually inflates until it looks like a large balloon. This stands out all the more because the color of the sac, which is red with occasional black spots, is in sharp contrast to the birds' shiny black feathers.

Looking for love in the skies, the males sit on low-growing shrubs and wait in anticipation of females that may fly by. When a female appears overhead, the males use more than their puffed-up good looks to attract her. With upturned heads, they shake their outstretched wings from side to side and make an ear-splitting cry that sounds like a repeated "woo-woo-woo-woo!" One shrill cry after another fills the air as the males strive to attract the attention of the flying females.

If one of the female birds finds the display worthy of her attention, she may decide to descend for a better look at the available males. Often the male birds congregate in groups and a female has her pick of the best and most attractive when she comes down for a closer look. The larger the red throat sac, the more attractive a male bird is to the females. Although a female chooses only one of the males, the rejected suitors do not seem to mind, and there is no fighting among the competing males.

Feathery Families

After a pair of frigate birds mates, they build their nest. Both the male and female birds gather twigs to construct their nest—usually on top of low-growing shrubbery. The female lays one egg in this nest. During incubation, which lasts about one-and-one-half months, both the male and the female share the job of protecting the egg. While the male is waiting to become a father, his bright red, puffy throat gradually begins to deflate. Finally, there is nothing but a small patch of skin left on his throat.

When the solitary chick hatches, both parents watch over it to guard against natural predators, such as owls and Galápagos hawks, which are fierce hunters. Another source of danger for

Female (left) *and male* (right) *frigate birds both sit on their nest.*

both eggs and chicks is other frigate birds, which will eat their own kind if given a chance.

Frigate birds do not gain independence from their parents quickly. It takes months before they learn to fly. Even after that, they may spend more than a year with their parents, learning how to hunt and fish so they can live safely on their own.

Introduced Threats

According to Dr. Carlos A. Valle, professor of ecology and conservation biology at the University of San Francisco de Quito in Ecuador, adult frigate birds are top predators in the islands and

This male frigate bird watches over his chick. The red on his throat is reduced to only a patch by the time the chick is born.

have no specific natural enemies. However, he found that rats attack frigate birds that nest close to the ground. Dr. Valle also noted that a breeding colony in Cerro Tijeretas on Isabela was abandoned nearly twenty years ago because the local people frequently disturbed the birds. Conservationists also wonder whether tourism could be a threat to these graceful birds, especially during the earlier parts of the year when courting and breeding occur on such widespread areas of the islands.

Yet another cause for concern is the possible effect of illegal fishing in the Galápagos. One type of commercial fishing, called long-lining, involves the use of fishing lines that are miles long and covered with many hooks. When these lines are cast into the ocean, some seabirds, such as the frigate birds, are attracted by the bait on the end of the hooks. When they attempt to eat the bait, the birds get caught on the hooks and drown.

El Niño

One natural threat to the frigate birds in the Galápagos happens in those years when a climatic condition called El Niño occurs in the waters surrounding the islands. El Niño, Spanish for "the infant," refers to the Christ child, because it usually happens around Christmastime. During an El Niño year, rainfall in the Galápagos is abnormally heavy, and air and water temperatures rise. This results in the lush growth of plants and other positive effects for animals on land, but El Niño causes many problems for seafaring creatures.

Because many species of fish and other marine animals in the Galápagos can live only in relatively cool water, the sudden rise in ocean temperature causes a destructive chain reaction among these animals. Plankton—tiny plant or animal organisms that float in the water—die out because the waters are too warm. As a result, many fish die of starvation because they cannot find plankton to eat. This in turn leads to seabirds, such as frigate birds, dying of starvation or attempting to fly far away to find food.

Trouble in the Skies

Although the frigate birds on the islands do not seem to be threatened with extinction, some other bird species in the Galápagos appear to be in trouble, and conservationists are concerned. The dark-rumped petrel, also called the Hawaiian petrel, is in serious danger. It is the only endangered bird species

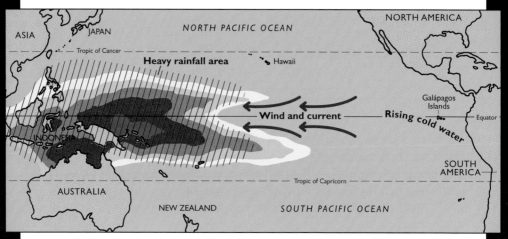

When El Niño is not present, the warmest waters in the Pacific Ocean are in the west, where rainfall is heavy. Near the equator, winds and ocean currents move from east to west. Cold, nutrient-rich water rises to the surface in the east (to replace water that flows away), supporting a large population of fish.

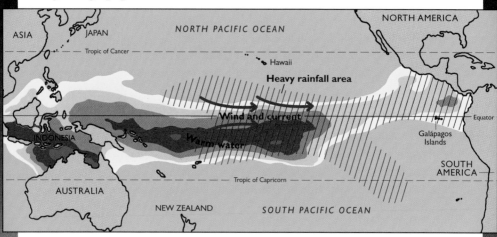

When El Niño is present, the east-to-west winds and currents weaken and sometimes reverse. The pattern of heavy rainfall then shifts eastward. The fish population declines in the east because the cold water no longer rises to the surface there.

This young dark-rumped petrel rests in the nest where it was born. Its feathers will turn black and white as it matures.

in the Galápagos Islands. Feral cats, dogs, rats, and pigs eat both young and adult petrels. A smaller version of this species is in even greater danger in Hawaii, where it is close to extinction, because of animals that were introduced to those islands.

The dark-rumped petrel in the Galápagos is about 15 inches long from bill to tail. It has mostly white feathers on its underside, but its back, the top of its head, its upper wings, and its tail are black. It is a nocturnal seabird that eats fish and other marine creatures, especially squid. These petrels live almost everywhere in the archipelago and spend much of their time flying above the ocean in search of food.

Every year the petrels leave their ocean hunting grounds and nest in long burrows in the moist soil in the highlands of Floreana, San Cristóbal, Santa Cruz, and Isabela. After mating, the female petrel lays only one egg. This makes the species even more vulnerable. If the birds laid more eggs, there would be a higher chance of survival for each generation. If a mother petrel's only

Beautiful, colorful greater flamingos (top) *grace the waters around Santa Cruz Island. Populations of birds such as the blue-footed booby* (bottom right) *and the waved albatross* (bottom left) *are being reduced by fishers who practice illegal long-line fishing.*

egg is destroyed or eaten, she won't lay another one until the following year. The parents leave the chicks by themselves for days at a time while they fly off to hunt for food. While the parents are away, the chicks are vulnerable to predators.

When settlers came to the islands, they planted crops in the volcanic soil where the dark-rumped petrels nested, destroying many nesting sites. The settlers' animals, too, hunted petrel eggs, chicks, and even adult birds.

Only in the 1960s did scientists realize how desperate the situation was for these petrels. They found that on Santa Cruz only four nests out of ninety-two successfully produced young petrels. To help this situation, in 1982 the CDRS and the GNPS created a predator control program in the dark-rumped petrel colony in Cerro Pajas on Floreana. They set up poisoned bait to kill rats and cats. As a result, eight out of ten petrel chicks make it to adulthood on the island.

There is also a program on the island of Santiago to eliminate pigs that prey upon the dark-rumped petrel. Future programs will keep dogs and cats out of the petrel breeding grounds on Santa Cruz.

Impact of Introduced Animals

Other birds that have been affected by the human population or introduced animals include Galápagos rails, flamingos, and some mockingbirds. Many of the terrestrial, or land-dwelling, birds on San Cristóbal are endangered by introduced dogs and cats.

The mangrove finch, the smallest of the Galápagos finches, is endangered on Fernandina because fishers have been cutting down the mangrove trees that serve as the birds' habitat—the place where they normally live. On Isabela, where an estimated fifty pairs of mangrove finches live, a black rat was recently found in one of the nests.

The Galápagos rail, a land bird, is becoming increasingly difficult to find in the archipelago. According to Johannah Barry of the Charles Darwin Foundation (CDF), it may already be extinct on some of the islands.

In addition to the frigate birds, boobies and waved albatrosses have fallen prey to the hooks of illegal long-line fishing.

The waved albatrosses could be especially affected because they breed mainly on one island, Española. Any losses would greatly affect their population.

Dr. Linda Cayot, who worked at the CDRS and was a researcher in the Galápagos from 1981 until 1998, commented, "Albatrosses all over the world have been extremely affected by long-lining. If this type of fishing became legalized in the Galápagos, it would have the same major impact on these birds as in other places in the world."

Complicated Impacts

Flightless birds, such as the flightless cormorant and the Galápagos penguin, are susceptible to attacks by introduced ani-

A flightless cormorant flaps its wings.

The Galápagos Islands' natural beauty and unusual forms of wildlife are a big draw for tourists. These visitors embark on a tour of North Seymour Island.

mals. Both types of birds are endemic to the Galápagos and breed mostly in a relatively small area along the coastlines of Fernandina and Isabela. Because these birds have small populations in the archipelago, they are especially vulnerable.

Dr. Matthew James is one of the directors of the Galápagos Coalition, an organization formed in 1995 to study conservation issues in the archipelago. He explained that many birds continue to be indirectly affected by a series of events that

With an increasing human presence on the islands, dangers to the wildlife are evident. This sea lion has found a plastic bag that could get caught in the animal's throat and choke it.

starts with humans. "The rats in the Galápagos are a result of increased human presence in the islands," he said. "The more people there are that visit or live in the islands, the more chances there are for species to move from island to island or to introduce new species from the South American mainland or Asia or other locations."

He added that tourism provides increased income for the government of Ecuador, but there are also concerns associated with these visitors to the islands. "The more tourists you have," commented Dr. James, "the more restaurants and new T-shirt shops there will be." He added that tourism leads to more immigration of Ecuadoreans from the mainland. "The population of the mainland is growing 2 percent a year, but the population of the Galápagos is growing 8 percent a year."

When these new inhabitants look for work, it can have disastrous consequences on the fragile ecosystem, such as in the case of sea cucumber fishing. This industry has provided well-paid jobs for many Ecuadorean fishers, but has had negative effects on the environment.

One of the ways that fishers harvest sea cucumbers is by diving into the water and turning over rocks to look for them. This disturbs the ocean floor and affects the fish that live in the cracks and crevices of those rocks. Birds, such as the flightless cormorant, feed off those fish, so their food supply is disturbed. The fish, in turn, feed off small invertebrates (animals without a spinal column) that live on the rocks, and these, too, have their habitat disrupted or destroyed.

Dr. James commented, "Everything has an impact. The problems are a complicated set of interactions. They might start with economics but end up affecting the penguins and the flightless cormorants."

Chapter 4

Dragons of the Sea

The Galápagos Islands are home to marine iguanas—a kind of tropical lizard—that regularly dive to depths of more than 35 feet. Although they usually swim underwater for ten minutes or less, they can remain submerged for up to an hour while searching for red or green algae, their main sources of food. Algae is a type of seaweed. In the Galápagos, red and green algae grow on rocks in the ocean and are sometimes exposed to the air during low tide. Marine iguanas—with leathery skin and curved claws—look like diving dragons as they plunge into the ocean surf. They are seeking the salty meals that they scrape off rocks with their powerful jaws.

Iguanas can grow to a length of three feet. Visitors to the Galápagos Islands are often amazed at the tameness of these creatures. This author was running on black rocks on Santiago Island only to be stopped suddenly by the sight of dark-skinned iguanas that at first blended into the background. They continued sunbathing and were totally unconcerned to see a creature many times their size quickly advancing in their direction and almost stepping on them.

The iguana's dark skin is more than just an attractive covering. It helps these cold-blooded animals regulate their body temperature by absorbing heat. After a long dive in relatively

This marine iguana resembles a miniature dinosaur as it emerges from the sea. Its claws help it hang onto a rock until it dives into the water in search of more algae.

cool waters, marine iguanas can quickly soak up heat from the sun by basking on the rocks alongside the pounding surf.

During the breeding season, however, these dark skin tones change to bright colors that attract mates. Iguanas may turn shades of red, orange, or green to charm members of the opposite sex. Although both sexes change colors during mating season, the females change most during the egg-laying period. Since the females are often covered in dust and dirt from the nest-building process, the color change isn't always as obvious as it is in the males.

Built-in Heaters and Air Conditioners

Because marine iguanas are cold-blooded, they must rely on ingenious ways to maintain the right body temperature. In addition to their heat-absorbing dark color, they regulate their temperature by striking different postures that help them keep warmer or cooler.

For instance, on a day when there are no clouds in the sky, the sun beats down mercilessly on these reptiles. To keep their temperature from rising to dangerously high levels, marine iguanas raise themselves up on their front legs as they lie in the sun. This lifts the underside of the body away from the brutally hot lava formations that line the shore. As a result, air can circulate under the body, keeping it at a safe, constant temperature.

Survival of the Fittest

According to Darwin's theory of evolution, species that came to the harsh conditions of life in the Galápagos had to change or adapt to the unique features of the islands. Because there was so little fresh water or food, scientists believe that an ancestral iguana species from the mainland of Central or South America gradually changed some of its characteristics and behaviors as new generations were born.

The sharp, curved claws of marine iguanas provide one example of these adaptations. The claws are well adapted to hanging on to underwater rocks to avoid being swept away by strong undersea currents. The claws of land iguanas, which are not needed to hang on to rocks and vegetation, are smaller than those of their diving relatives.

The snout of the marine iguana has also evolved into a shape

The marine iguana's long, sharp claws and short snout help it to get algae off rocks.

different from that of its cousins on land. Because the snout is shorter, it is easier for the marine iguana to find seaweed that grows on underwater rocks.

Its tail and body, too, show evidence of adaptation. The marine iguana needs to swim for its supper. Its thin but powerful tail can propel the animal through the water quickly and aid its underwater search for food. Its body gracefully bends and curves as it swims.

Sneezing Salt

One of the most amazing adaptations that marine iguanas have made is in the way they obtain drinking water. Because fresh water is so scarce on the islands, these dragonlike lizards have adapted to drinking seawater. Their food, too, whether on rocks near the shore or underwater, is naturally seasoned with large amounts of salt.

How do these iguanas rid their bodies of so much excess salt? Above their eyes, they have special glands connected internally to their nostrils. They use these specialized glands to push out the excess salt that they have amassed from their ocean diet. If you go to the Galápagos and observe marine iguanas, you may think that they are sneezing frequently, but they are not.

Marine iguanas allow some of the resident animals on the islands to help them stay clean and well groomed. Galápagos ground finches eat ticks off the skin of marine iguanas. Tiny lava lizards run and jump on marine iguanas and are rewarded with a tasty meal of insects or a piece of dead skin. Occasionally a bright orange and yellow Sally Lightfoot crab will saunter over the scaly skin of a marine iguana, only to be ignored by the menacing-looking but harmless reptile.

Marine iguanas coexist peacefully with fellow Galápagos wildlife, such as Sally Lightfoot crabs (above left).

Raising a Scaly Family

Marine iguanas breed at different times on different islands, but most of them mate at the beginning of the year. When the mating season starts, male iguanas begin to stake out their territories. They are often competitive with other males. They pose in threatening postures and nod their heads up and down to show their aggression. The crest, the showy tuft on the back of an iguana's neck, becomes tall and erect. The reptile stands with his tail down and his mouth partly open to show his rivals the menacing red color inside his mouth.

Usually the males do not attack one another, but in some instances they fight by butting each other with their heads. These aggressive behaviors may continue for hours until one male becomes tired and retreats.

When a male has won over a territory from his rivals, he tries to attract a female to his area. He will walk around her in a circle and nod his head quickly. If he is successful in mating with her, he may continue on and try to breed with other females during the same mating season.

After a female has mated, she lays her eggs in the sand. Females look for suitable places to dig burrows to lay their eggs. When they have deposited up to four eggs in their burrow, they seal them with sand and guard these sites to make sure that other iguanas do not dig them up.

Two to four months later, the newborn marine iguanas hatch and dig themselves out of the burrows. This is a dangerous time for the vulnerable hatchlings because some natural predators of the marine iguana exist on the islands. Galápagos snakes, although small and nonpoisonous, capture and devour young iguanas. The Galápagos hawk—one of the strongest hunters—and seabirds such as herons and lava gulls, also prey on hatchlings.

On Hood Island, this female marine iguana is digging a burrow where she will lay her eggs.

Effects of El Niño

The greatest destruction of marine iguanas, however, happens when there is an occurrence of El Niño, the climatic feature that warms the waters surrounding the islands. The worst El Niño ever recorded occurred between 1982 and 1983. This dramatic rise in ocean temperature—about 10 degrees—led to unusual developments on land. Finches that normally breed only after the age of one year were recorded as breeding just after they were four months old. The El Niño led to devastation of the marine iguana population on some islands. Researchers estimated that at least 70 percent of all the marine iguanas living on Santa Fé died.

Although predators and temperature swings can decimate marine iguana populations, neither of these natural factors has the potential to do as much harm as one introduced species—humans. Marine iguanas thrive throughout most of the archipelago. They seem to be in trouble on some islands, however, including Santa Cruz and San Cristóbal. Dr. Linda Cayot stated that these iguanas are in trouble on the islands populated by humans because pet cats escaped in the past and formed a wild population that preys upon iguanas. She explained, "Cats are one of the introduced species that are the most difficult to get rid of. Although we control cats in land iguana nesting areas, the marine iguanas are so dispersed that it would be very costly and time-consuming to eradicate them [cats] completely."

Dragons of the Land

Iguanas are also found on dry land in the Galápagos. Although similar reptiles in varying forms live in other countries, the land iguanas in the Galápagos Islands are not found anywhere else in the world. In fact, Dr. Cayot explained that all of the terrestrial reptiles in the Galápagos are endemic.

These land relatives of marine iguanas live on dry areas in several islands in the archipelago. Unlike marine iguanas, they cannot dive or drink saltwater. Since almost no freshwater is found on the majority of the islands, the land iguanas must quench their thirst by eating foods that contain moisture. The succulent fruits of the opuntia, or prickly pear cactus, contain a large amount of water. The land iguana has a strong, sturdy mouth that helps it get past the sharp thorns of the cactus fruits.

When ripe fruits drop to the ground, hungry and thirsty land iguanas take advantage of this combined food and drink. They either take cautious bites between the thorns or roll the fruits around on the ground until most of the thorns are worn off. The iguanas' reward is a tasty, juicy mouthful. Occasionally, a land iguana may accidentally chew on unavoidable thorns, but the lizard's powerful jaws can crush them without the thorns causing permanent injury to the animal.

Galápagos land iguanas have some physical differences that distinguish them from their seagoing cousins. Their colors are usually brighter than those of the marine variety. They may be intense shades of yellow or orange as opposed to the generally muted tones of marine iguanas. Like their cousins in the water, however, newly born land iguanas often fall prey to predatory birds, such as hawks and owls.

The Iguanas of Baltra

One of the most interesting populations of Galápagos land

Land iguanas feed on cactus plants. This land iguana is eating an opuntia cactus.

iguanas originated on Baltra, a flat, dry island that belongs to the Ecuadorean military. Baltra, which is not part of the Galápagos National Park system, once was home to a native population that included the largest land iguanas in the Galápagos Islands.

In 1932, U.S. researchers from a scientific expedition called the Hancock Expedition observed the Baltra iguanas and noted that they were underweight. They also observed that there was a large goat population on the island and that vegetation had been destroyed by these feral animals.

Just north of Baltra lies an island called North Seymour. At the time of the expedition, there were no land iguanas living there. Noting that the vegetation on North Seymour was similar to that on Baltra, the U.S. scientists decided to try an experiment. They transplanted about seventy land iguanas from Baltra to North Seymour in 1932 and 1933. However, the scientists never went back to check on the population.

Years later, when World War II broke out, the United States opened a military base on Baltra to protect the Panama Canal. During that time, more than one thousand military personnel lived on the island, and houses were built for these residents. There was a decree that no animals on the island could be killed, so the goat population continued to grow. After World War II, the land iguanas of Baltra became extinct, probably as a result of habitat destruction, the presence of the military base, and the destructive effects of the feral goat population.

In the 1970s, scientists showed a renewed interest in the land iguanas that remained on North Seymour. They found cause for concern because they observed that there was little reproduction among these reptiles, and the iguana population was declining.

In 1980 scientists brought one pair of land iguanas from North Seymour into captivity and bred them. After that, more pairs were brought in until there were enough young iguanas to start a repatriation program in Baltra. (A repatriation program sends captive-bred animals back to the islands that they originally came from.) However, there was a delay in going ahead with this project because Baltra belongs to the Ecuadorean military, and it was not as easy as repatriating them into the areas of the Galápagos Islands that are part of the national park system.

Finally in 1991, an agreement was signed between the CDF, the Ecuadorean Ministry of Agriculture (which was in charge of the GNPS at the time), and the Ecuadorean Air Force, which was in charge of Baltra. The repatriation began, and the CDF got permission to continue to travel to and work on Baltra to monitor the iguana population.

That year, thirty-five land iguanas were brought to the island. By 1997, six years later, almost ninety iguanas lived there—providing evidence that some natural reproduction was occurring among the repatriated iguanas. Because the program proved so successful, it is ongoing.

The population may have also been helped by the powerful El Niño of the early 1980s, which generally helps land animals in the Galápagos because of the increase in rain and the consequent growth of vegetation. Dr. Cayot cautioned, however, "We need twenty or thirty years to be able to say that this program is a success. We can't just say in five or ten years that this is working and take the land iguanas off North Seymour." The program seems to have been a success because of the hatching iguanas, but only time will tell if this success will continue.

Chapter 5

Preserving Nature's Diversity

Will the unique species of flora and fauna in the Galápagos archipelago survive the presence of humans? Can the native species adapt to the foreign plants and animals that people accidentally or purposely introduce to the islands? Will iguanas, tortoises, and some birds die out if cats, goats, and pigs destroy their sources of food and eat their young? Will established species be brought to the brink of extinction?

Some people think that the only way to protect these priceless plants and animals is through international cooperation. The Ecuadorean government must join forces with other countries to help eradicate the introduced plants and animals that threaten the continued existence of the native species.

A Park Made of Islands

In 1959 the government of Ecuador declared 95 percent of the Galápagos Islands a national park. That year marked the one-hundredth anniversary of the publication of Charles Darwin's *On the Origin of Species*. Since 1968 the government of Ecuador has actively managed the islands through its Galápagos National Park Service.

In 1986 Ecuador established the Galápagos Marine

The government of Ecuador is trying to protect the Galápagos archipelago while allowing people to enjoy its beauty. Here, tourists hike on lush San Cristóbal Island.

Resources Reserve (GMRR), which encompasses many of the waters near and surrounding the islands. This is one of the largest protected marine areas in the world, second only to the Great Barrier Reef in Australia. In addition, when Ecuador was a member of the International Whaling Commission in 1990, Rodrigo Borja Cevallos, the Ecuadorean president at the time, declared the waters of the GMRR a whale sanctuary.

To ensure that the Galápagos Islands remain pristine, and to avoid the introduction of foreign plants and animals, the national park system established several rules that are strictly enforced by park wardens and guides. For instance, groups of tourists to the islands must be accompanied by certified guides who have been trained to stay on the designated trails and to keep conservation in mind at all times. Visitors may not take any kind of food or drink to the islands. If food contained insects, these unwanted creatures might thrive in the area and cause problems. The introduction of an unwanted plant species could occur if a visitor dropped a piece of fruit and its seeds grew.

Some of the most important park rules concern the animals themselves. Because most animals in the islands are so tame, they will not run or fly away from tourists. Inconsiderate visitors could easily disturb or chase these animals, so the national park service strictly forbids these behaviors. In addition, visitors must not touch the animals. As tempting as it is to reach out and pet these gentle creatures, doing so could cause them to lose their tameness around humans. Visitors must also refrain from feeding the animals. This could not only harm them, but might also cause them to stop looking for their natural food sources.

Littering is also prohibited. Although food and drinks are forbidden, some people might sneak them in. Cans that are carelessly thrown away can cut unsuspecting animals such as sea lions, and plastic can be mistaken for food. Sea turtles attempting to eat plastic articles could choke and die. Any items that don't belong in this fragile environment could harm the balance of nature.

The Charles Darwin Foundation

In 1959, at the same time the GNPS was formed, the CDF for the Galápagos Islands was also created. It was formed with the cooperation of the Ecuadorean government, the International Union for Conservation of Nature and Natural Resources (since renamed the World Conservation Union), and UNESCO (the United Nations Educational, Scientific, and Cultural Organization).

The purpose of the CDF is to act as an adviser to the Ecuadorean government with regard to conservation issues on the islands. To carry out this goal, the CDF operates the CDRS on Santa Cruz to aid scientific research in the Galápagos Islands.

The CDF has developed public environmental education programs both locally and internationally. In addition, the organization helps to raise money for research and conservation programs. The CDF also trains Ecuadorean scientists.

Breeding Programs

Since the CDF and the GNPS were created, many conservation programs that combine wildlife management and research have been instituted. Their success has been extraordinary. The breeding and repatriation program at the CDRS has had the

The CDRS on Santa Cruz Island protects and breeds giant tortoises.

highest success rate of any such program in the world. The tortoises in the program, for example, have had a 50 percent hatching rate and a 97 percent survival rate. That means that half of the eggs that tortoises lay actually hatch, and for every hundred eggs that hatch, ninety-seven baby tortoises survive to adulthood.

In 1959, when the GNPS was first established, researchers started to observe the tortoise populations. They were startled to find that there were no juvenile or young adult tortoises on the island of Pinzón. The population consisted solely of adults that were about 100 to 150 years old. Of these, two were males and fourteen were females. The problem was that rats were killing all of the hatchlings in their nests.

A program was started on the island of Pinzón to save the endangered tortoises. Beginning in the early 1980s, the CDRS eradicated the rats from the island. The tortoises were successfully repatriated.

Giant tortoises live in the wild and at the CDRS. Visitors to the research station can get an up-close look at these remarkable, dinosaurlike creatures.

After these baby tortoises hatched, they were released in the wild.

On the island of Española, only a few tortoises were found in the 1970s, and they were spread out around the island. It would be difficult for slow-moving males and females to meet each other on this large island, and then to mate and produce young. To help them find each other, researchers took these isolated tortoises off the island and brought them to the CDRS to breed. The research station instituted a subsequent program in the 1980s to eradicate rats that threatened the remaining tortoises on this island.

After the rats were removed from Española, the tortoises and their new hatchlings were repatriated. Thanks to the breeding and repatriation program, the original survivors of this area are now the grandparents of a whole new generation of healthy tortoises that are not in danger of predation (being captured and eaten) by rats.

On Santiago the tortoise population had dwindled to five hundred, and most of these were males. To make matters worse, the feral goat and pig populations exploded in the nineteenth century. One theory is that fishers left goats and pigs on this island so they could be insured a steady supply of meat when they returned. Over time, the pigs and goats multiplied. Starting in the 1970s, the park and station worked for more than twenty years to drive down the pig population. In 1997 it appeared that most of the pigs had been eliminated from the area.

The tortoise population on Santa Cruz was a healthy one, with more than three thousand animals. Because pigs preyed on the nests, however, the tortoises are threatened. In the early 1980s, the research center started collecting eggs to breed in captivity to solve this problem.

Volcan Alcedo on Isabela was the focus of a program to eliminate feral goats that threatened tortoises breeding on the rim of the volcano. The tortoises had less food, water, and shelter on this volcano as a result of the goats' enormous appetites. In order to remedy this problem, at the end of 1996, the CDRS and the GNPS instituted a multimillion-dollar program to get rid of the goats on Alcedo. This involved shooting the goats. The station asked for expertise from conservationists in the United States and New Zealand, where such programs have been instituted in the past because of similar problems with introduced animals.

Learning from Conservation Efforts

Dr. Cayot, the coordinator of the Isabela project, explained that researchers in the program have learned much since its beginning. She said that in the early years of the program, the researchers had a long-term vision, and they started a program that has been extremely successful. They went to troubled areas and looked for nests to bring back eggs or hatchlings. The tortoises were raised until they were three or four years old. At this age, a tortoise's shell is hard enough to prevent rats from eating

Giant tortoises are cared for at the CDRS. These tortoises chew on stalks while visitors study their movements.

it and the tortoise is also less vulnerable to natural problems such as droughts.

Dr. Cayot said, "A lot of what they did in the early years didn't work well. Researchers brought the eggs back early in the season when they shouldn't be moved, so they weren't able to develop. But bit by bit, through trial and error, they learned, and the program improved."

The programs are continually being refined as researchers gain the experience needed to deal with these ecological issues. Scientists look at the problems from a management perspective. They must study many aspects of the individual situations to decide what should be done first. For instance, if an island ecosystem is threatened by both pigs and goats, which animal should the station target first? Goats eat immense amounts of foliage. If the goats are shot and eradicated first, however, the pigs will have more places to hide. This makes them more difficult to find, and they might continue to thrive in the area. A more logical step might be for the scientists to eradicate the pigs first.

Science and Management

Dr. Cayot explained that in the 1960s and early 1970s, conservation efforts consisted of bringing twenty to fifty young tortoises to the CDRS at a time. Efforts have since increased to accommodate up to seven hundred tortoises at a time. "We're moving them through and getting them back out to the islands that they came from," she said.

"It's extremely successful and the key to all of this is the combination of science and management. The whole time we're trying to save these animals, we're doing experiments to keep improving how we do it so that we get better and better at it. The breeding center for tortoises now has a regular system and doesn't need a lot of improvement," she concluded.

Computers and Conservation

You will probably never see live reptiles on sale in your supermarket, but the bar code technology that helps ring up prices on a cash register has made it easier to keep track of tortoises in

Young tortoises gather to munch on huge leaves.

the CDRS and in their natural habitat. Edward Louis is the geneticist at the Henry Doorly Zoo who worked with Jeremy Taylor and Scott Davis to find a mate for Lonesome George. Dr. Louis explained how "pit tags" are used to identify some animals in the Galápagos.

In 1991 Dr. Louis and his associates did the first pit tagging of tortoises on the Galápagos Islands. Using special needles, they injected one microchip—a bit longer than a grain of rice— into the left back leg of each of the tortoises in the program. As the needle goes under the skin of the animal, a small plunger inserts the microchip into the animal's muscle.

Dr. Louis explained that this method is superior to tagging animals with radio collars, which can fall off. The microchip does not harm the animal and can remain within its body indefinitely. When scientists want to positively identify an animal, they run a scanner past the tortoise's leg. A number is displayed on the scanner. When this is looked up in a database, the identity of the tortoise is immediately revealed.

In the early 1990s, Dr. Louis, his team, and people from the CDRS worked together and injected pit tags in all the animals in captivity at the CDRS. In addition, they tagged some of the wild populations living on Volcan Wolf. This helps scientists to keep track of the age and location of the animals.

Future of the Islands

What will happen to these islands in the future? What would it mean if different animal and plant species die out? Tom Fritts, a research biologist, commented, "When you lose a species, it is gone forever. Each of these species is a living, breathing organism. They have been here for thousands if not millions of years,

Oil began leaking from the tanker Jessica *on Friday, January 19, 2001, two days after the vessel ran aground off the coast of San Cristóbal Island. The resulting oil spill threatened the delicate marine life in the area and the entire food chain of the rare species living on the Galápagos Islands.*

and to rub them out like a chalk drawing is something that has a major effect on humankind."

Fritts went on to say that each species can be viewed as an experiment in its environment, and it would be unfortunate to see a species destroyed before scientists have a chance to see how it would ultimately evolve. "If we view the earth as an organism," he said, "then each one of these component species is like one of its vital organs." He concluded, "We need international cooperation to help Ecuador save the Galápagos from ruination, and we have to view it as a world heritage, not just a national heritage."

Never was that more true than in January 2001, when an Ecuadorean oil tanker, the *Jessica,* ran aground off San Cristóbal Island and started leaking fuel. The tanker, on a regular supply run to meet the needs of the increasing human population on the islands, was loaded with 240,000 gallons of diesel fuel and fuel oil. About two-thirds of the cargo spilled into the ocean.

Eduadorean environment minister Rodolfo Rendón said, "The situation is very, very severe. . . . We'll need all the national and international help we can get." In response, teams of volunteers from around the world flocked to the area to bring injured animals to impromptu veterinary stations. The Ecuadorean navy worked around the clock, and a team of U.S. Coast Guard specialists worked with local officials to minimize the impact of the spill, which threatened the fragile ecosystem.

Saving nature's diversity in the archipelago is the responsibility of everyone who lives on this earth. We must all support continued conservation programs to ensure that the Galápagos will remain "the living laboratory of evolution" that they were when Charles Darwin first visited these seemingly magical islands.

Glossary

algae: a group of simple plantlike organisms that have no true root, stem, or leaf and often grow in colonies in water or on damp surfaces

archipelago: a group or chain of islands

biodiversity: the variety of different life-forms living in an area

core: the intensely hot innermost part of the earth

creationism: the theory that all living things were directly created by God and essentially remain the way they were created

crust: the hard outer layer of the earth that lies above the core and the mantle

endemic: native to a particular place or region; refers to plants or animals that are found only in one area

equator: an imaginary circle around the middle of the earth, at an equal distance from the North Pole and the South Pole. The equator divides the earth into the Northern Hemisphere and the Southern Hemisphere.

evolution: the theory that all plants and animals have developed from earlier forms by gradual change over periods of many years

feral: having escaped from domestication and become wild

hot spot: an area in the earth's mantle layer that contains great concentrations of heat

lava: molten rock that flows from volcanoes

mantle: the part of the earth that lies outside the core and under the crust. The mantle is about 1,800 miles thick.

natural selection: the theory describing a process in nature by which the organisms best suited to their environment are the ones most likely to survive and reproduce. The theory of natural selection was first explained in detail in the 1850s by the British naturalist Charles R. Darwin. It is also called "survival of the fittest."

nocturnal: active at night

paleontologist: a scientist who studies the life of past geological periods from fossil remains

plankton: tiny plant or animal organisms that float in a body of water and provide food for fish and other animals

tectonic plates: large plates that consist of part of the earth's crust and a portion of the upper part of the mantle. The plates move about slowly on molten rock in the mantle. Many of these plates are under both ocean floor and dry land. Some plates hold entire continents.

Selected Bibliography

Darwin, Charles. *On the Origin of Species.* 1859. Reprint, New York: Random House, 1993.

_____. *Voyage of the Beagle.* N. d. Reprint, New York: Penguin Books, 1989.

Hunt, Carla. "Galápagos—Fights to Preserve Natural Attraction." *Travel Weekly,* September 11, 1995.

Jackson, Michael H. *Galápagos—A Natural History.* Calgary, Alberta, Canada: University of Calgary Press, 1995.

Lemonick, Michael D. "Can the Galápagos Survive?" *Time,* October 30, 1995.

Myers, Lynne Born, and Christopher A. Myers. *Galápagos—Islands of Change.* New York: Hyperion Books for Children, 1995.

Schafer, Susan. *The Galápagos Tortoise.* New York: Dillon Press, 1992.

Selsam, Millicent E. *Land of the Giant Tortoise—The Story of Galápagos.* New York: Four Winds Press, 1977.

Steadman, David W., and Steven Zousmer. *Galápagos—Discovery on Darwin's Islands.* Washington, D.C.: Smithsonian Institution Press, 1988.

Thornton, Ian. *Darwin's Islands—A Natural History of Galápagos.* New York: The Natural History Press, 1971.

"Too Many People: Galápagos." *The Economist,* May 10, 1997.

Internet Resources

Charles Darwin Foundation and the Charles Darwin Research Station
<http://www.darwinfoundation.org>
A large site with information about the geography and wildlife of the Galápagos Islands, plus a brief biography of Charles Darwin, information about the Charles Darwin Research Station and its projects, news from the Galápagos, and a special area just for kids

Discovery Channel School: Explore Galápagos <http://school.discovery.com/schooladventures/galapagos>
Fun facts, games, and quizzes about the Galápagos

Galápagos.org <http://www.galapagos.org>
Information about the Charles Darwin Foundation and how to join, articles about current issues and news in the Galápagos, a full-color photo gallery, and answers to frequently asked questions about the Galápagos

Galápagos Coalition <http://www.law.emory.edu/PI/GALAPAGOS>
Information about the various organizations for the protection of the Galápagos Islands, legal and environmental issues in the Galápagos, several maps, and links to related sites

Galápagos Conservation Trust <http://www.gct.org>
A useful site with information on how to join the Conservation Trust, current challenges facing the Galápagos, news, travel information, and general facts about the islands

Galápagos Island Wildlife Refuge at Cyber Nation Interactive
<http://www.spacelab.net/~cni>
A fun, graphics-heavy site including information about the wildlife of the islands, a large photo gallery, maps, and even a quiz to test your knowledge of the Galápagos

GalápagosQuest <http://quest.classroom.com/archive/galapagosquest1999/pg02604.htm>
Packed with details about history, wildlife, and geography, this site re-creates an expedition to the Galápagos Islands, complete with daily reports, photos, and maps

iExplore: The Galápagos Islands <http://www.iexplore.com/multimedia/galapagos.jhtml>
A multimedia introduction to the islands and their inhabitants, presented by National Geographic

Virtual Galápagos <http://terraquest.com/galapagos>
A highly interactive site that chronicles a trip to the Galápagos by the TerraQuest team. Maps, photos, and reports from the field allow you to experience the journey while gathering facts about the plants, animals, and history of the islands. A special section for students and teachers includes information about further research and ideas for classroom projects.

For Further Reading and Viewing

BOOKS

Blashfield, Jean F. *Galápagos Islands.* Austin, TX: Raintree Steck-Vaughn Publishers, 1995.

De Roy, Tui. *Galápagos: Islands Born of Fire.* Shrewsbury, U.K.: Swan Hill Press, 1998.

Evans, J. Edward. *Charles Darwin: Revolutionary Biologist.* Minneapolis: Lerner Publications Company, 1993.

Gelman, Rita Golden. *From Dawn to Dusk in the Galápagos: Flightless Birds, Swimming Lizards, and Other Fascinating Creatures.* Boston: Little, Brown and Company, 1991.

Melville, Herman, with an introduction, critical epilogue, and bibliographical notes by Victor Wolfgang Von Hagen. *The Encantadas, or Enchanted Isles.* N. d. Reprint, Burlingame, CA: William P. Wreden, 1940.

VIDEOS

Audubon Video. *Galápagos: My Fragile World.* Photographed by Tui De Roy. Vestron Video. 1986.

Discovery Channel Video. *Galápagos: Beyond Darwin.* Produced and directed by Al Giddings and David Clark. 100 min. 1996.

National Geographic Video. *Galápagos Islands: Land of Dragons.* N.d.

PBS Home Video. *In the Wild: Galápagos Islands with Richard Dreyfuss.* 60 min. 1996.

Index

About the Author

Linda Tagliaferro is a writer and illustrator whose previous Lerner Publications books include *Destination New York, Genetic Engineering: Progress or Peril?*, and *Bruce Lee*, a biography. Linda is a regular contributor to the *New York Times,* and she has written for numerous newspapers and magazines.

Linda was born in Brooklyn, New York, and has lived and studied in Denmark, Italy, and Indonesia. She has traveled extensively through Europe, Asia, Africa, South America, and the Caribbean. Linda lives in Little Neck, New York, with her husband and teenage son.

Photo Acknowledgments

The visuals in this book are used with the permission of: Visuals Unlimited: (© Barbara Gerlach) pp. 1, 59, (© Gerald & Buff Corsi) pp. 26, 33, 40, 42, 50 (bottom), 52, 56, 62, (© Jeff Greenberg) pp. 29 (top), 53, 72, 73, (© David Cavagnaro) p. 29 (bottom), (© Robin Karpan) p. 68, (© Joe McDonald) p. 76; © Wolfgang Kaehler, pp. 2-3, 6, 9, 12, 14-15, 16, 18, 23, 24, 30, 36, 45, 46, 48, 50 (top), 54, 61, 65; American Philosophical Society, p. 8; North Wind Picture Archives, p. 10; Corbis: (© Bettman) p. 12 (top), (© Academy of Natural Sciences of Philadelphia) p. 12 (bottom); © Al Giddings/Al Giddings Images, Inc., p. 19; Cleveland Health Services Library/Allen Memorial Library, p. 20; Smithsonian Institution, p. 21; Charles Darwin Research Station, pp. 37, 38, 74; © Miguel Castro/The National Audubon Society Collection/Photo Researchers, p. 49; Dr. Ed Louis/Henry Doorly Zoo, p. 78; AP Wide World Photos, p. 80.

Front cover: © Wolfgang Kaehler (right, left, background); © David Cavagnaro/ Visuals Unlimited (center)
Back cover: Library of Congress